FOR THE PEOPLE..

The
Kansas Bill Of Rights

From The Kansas Constitution

Preface & facts by
Tiano Bey

Additional copies of the pocket edition can be
purchased upon request email

PREFACE

If you live in the State of Kansas it is important that you know about the rights guaranteed to you in these political borders. No matter where you live or how you feel about it, ignorance of the law is no excuse. If we hope to make the place we call home a better environment where happiness can be pursued unmolested. We must first do our part in order to protect those rights that would create such a place. Today every household should have a copy of their **States Constitution** and a **law dictionary** for the purpose of interpretation. Government is the child of the people. And without the proper supervision, it can mature into an oppressive extension. **Freedom** is only as important as you make it. Its time you Make it a priority.

KANSAS GOVERNMENT

Regardless of your political affiliation Kansas is guaranteed a **republican form of government** as a condition of statehood. It is up to the people to maintain this reality.

KANSAS STATE FLAG

Adopted June 30ᵗʰ 1963

This design, without the word "Kansas",was
adopted on March 23ʳᵈ 1927

State Capital: City of Topeka

Governor: Laura Kelly

Lieutenant Governor: David Toland

Attorney Gen: Derek Schmidt

State Treasurer: Lynne Rodgers

Insurance Commissioner: Vicki Schmidt

Us Senators: Jerry Moran, Rodger Marshall

Us House Delegation: Tracy Mann, Jake Laturner, Sharice Davids and Ron Estes

KANSAS FACTS

1. **Who was the first person to Discover Kansas?**

   The first person to set foot in present day Kansas Was a Pawnee Moor by the name **El Turco**. In 1541 El Turco severed as an expedition adviser for the Spanish conquistador Francisco Vasquez de Coronado.

2. **How did Kansas become a possession of the United States?**

   In 1803 the United States acquired a portion of North America from France which became known as **The Louisiana Purchase**. With this purchase of new territory, The United States was able to more than double its size for only 15 million dollars. With all the controversy surrounding the authority of President Jefferson to make such a purchase on behalf of such an infant nation. The battle to protect and preserve the new territory was always on. From 1820-1854 the land that would soon become Kansas was largely considered a great desert, assumed only to be inhabitable by the so called "Indian".

3. When was Kansas admitted into the Union?

After a series of border wars known as the **Bleeding of Kansas**. The Kansas territory would be admitted into the Union as a **Free State under the Wyandotte Constitution** January 29th 1861. Making Kansas the 34th State.

4. Whose job is it to enforce the Constitution of Kansas?

The responsibility of enforcing the constitution of this state belongs to **The People** and those who they choose collectively to represent and protect their rights and interest.

5. When was the last time the Kansas Bill of Rights was amendment?

The Kansas Bill of Rights was last amended in 2016 for the purpose of **sec 21**. It has been said that the Kansas Constitution you see today is only a shell of what once was **THE ORIGINAL WYANDOTTE CONSTITUTION** of 1859. Since then the evolution of the Kansas Constitution has taken the shape of what is accepted by the Kansas resident of today, rather the incorporators.

PREAMBLE

We, **the people** of Kansas, grateful to Almighty God for our civil and religious privileges, in order to insure the full enjoyment of our **rights** as American citizens, do ordain and establish this constitution of the state of Kansas, with the following boundaries, to wit: Beginning at a point on the western boundary of the state of Missouri, where the thirty-seventh parallel of north latitude crosses the same; thence running west on said parallel to the twenty-fifth meridian of longitude west from Washington; thence north on said meridian to the fortieth parallel of north latitude; thence east on said parallel to the western boundary of the state of Missouri; thence south with the western boundary of said state to the place of beginning.

-The Kansas Constitution

KANSAS BILL OF RIGHTS

(EQUAL RIGHTS.)

§ 1. All men are possessed of equal and inalienable **natural rights**, among which are life, liberty, and the pursuit of happiness.

(POLITICAL POWER; PRIVILEGES)

§ 2. All political power is inherent in **the people**, and all free governments are founded on their authority, and are instituted for their equal protection and benefit. **No** special privileges or immunities shall ever be granted by the legislature, which may not be altered, revoked or repealed by the same body; and this power shall be exercised by no other tribunal or agency.

(RIGHT OF PEACEABLE ASSEMBLY; PETITION.)

§ 3. The people have the **right** to assemble, in a peaceable manner, to consult for their common good, to instruct their representatives, and to petition the government, or any department thereof, for the redress of grievances.

(INDIVIDUAL RIGHT TO BEAR ARMS; ARMIES.)

§ 4. A person has the **right** to keep and bear arms for the defense of self, family, home and state, for lawful hunting and recreational use, and for any other lawful purpose; but standing armies, in time of peace, are dangerous to liberty, and shall not be tolerated, and the military shall be in strict subordination to the civil power.

(TRIAL BY JURY)

§ 5. The **right** of trial by jury shall be inviolate.

(SLAVERY PROHIBITED; SERVITUDE FOR CONVICTION OF A CRIME.)

§ 6. There shall be **no** slavery in this state; and no involuntary servitude, **except** for the punishment of crime, whereof the party shall have been duly convicted.

(RELIGIOUS LIBERTY PROPERTY QUALIFICATION FOR PUBLIC OFFICE.)

§ 7. The **right** to worship God according to the dictates of conscience shall never be infringed; nor shall any person be compelled to attend or support any form of worship; nor shall any control of or interference with the rights of conscience be permitted, nor any preference be given by law to any religious establishment or mode of worship. **No** religious test or property qualification shall be required for any office of public trust, nor for any vote at any elections, nor shall any person be incompetent to testify on account of religious belief.

(HABEAS CORPUS)

§ 8. The <u>**right**</u> to the writ of habeas corpus shall not be suspended, unless the public safety requires it in case of invasion or rebellion.

§ 9. All persons shall be bailable by sufficient sureties except for capital offenses, where proof is evident or the presumption great. Excessive bail shall not be required, nor excessive fines imposed, nor cruel or unusual punishment inflicted.

§ 10. In all prosecutions, the accused shall be allowed to appear and defend in person, or by counsel; to demand the nature and cause of the accusation against him; to meet the witness face to face, and to have compulsory process to compel the attendance of the witnesses in his behalf, and a speedy public trial by an impartial jury of the county or district in which the offense is alleged to have been committed. **No** person shall be a witness against himself, or be twice put in jeopardy for the same offense.

§ 11. The liberty of the press shall be inviolate; and all persons may freely speak, write or publish their sentiments on all subjects, being responsible for the abuse of such rights; and in all civil or criminal actions for libel, the truth may be given in evidence to the jury, and if it shall appear that the alleged libelous matter was published for justifiable ends, the accused party shall be acquitted.

(NO FORFEITURE OF ESTATE FOR CRIMES).

§ 12. No conviction within the state shall work a forfeiture of estate.

(TREASON)

§ 13. Treason shall consist only in levying war against the state, adhering to its enemies, or giving them aid and comfort. **No** person shall be convicted of treason unless on the evidence of two witnesses to the overt act, or confession in open court.

(SOLDIERS' QUARTERS.)

§ 14. No soldier shall, in time of peace, be quartered in any house without the consent of the occupant, nor in time of war, except as prescribed by law.

(SEARCH AND SEIZURE.)

§ 15. The <u>right</u> of the people to be secure in their persons and property against unreasonable searches and seizures shall be inviolate; and **no** warrant shall issue but on probable cause, supported by oath or affirmation, particularly describing the place to be searched and the persons or property to be seized.

(IMPRISONMENT FOR DEBT.)

§ 16. **No** person shall be imprisoned for debt, except in cases of fraud.

(PROPERTY RIGHTS OF CITIZENS AND ALIENS)

§ 17. No distinction shall ever be made between citizens of the state of Kansas and the citizens of other states and territories of the United States in reference to the purchase, enjoyment or descent of property. The rights of aliens in reference to the purchase, enjoyment or descent of property may be regulated by law.

(JUSTICE WITHOUT DELAY.)

§ 18. All persons, for injuries suffered in person, reputation or property, shall have remedy by due course of law, and justice administered without delay.

(EMOLUMENTS OR PRIVILEGES PROHIBITED.)

§ 19. **No** hereditary emoluments, honors, or privileges shall ever be granted or conferred by the state.

(POWERS RETAINED BY PEOPLE.)

§ 20. This enumeration of rights shall not be construed to impair or deny others retained by the people; and all powers not herein delegated remain with the people.

(RIGHT OF PUBLIC TO HUNT, FISH AND TRAP WILDLIFE.)

§ 21. The people have **the right** to hunt, fish and trap, including by the use of traditional methods, subject to reasonable laws and regulations that promote wildlife conservation and management and that preserve the future of hunting and fishing. Public hunting and fishing shall be a preferred means of managing and controlling wildlife. This section shall not be construed to modify any provision of law relating to trespass, property rights or water resources.

Notes:

Notes:

Notes:

Notes:

Notes:

Notes:

Notes:

Notes:

www.ingramcontent.com/pod-product-compliance
Lightning Source LLC
Chambersburg PA
CBHW020333290526
45785CB00007B/3038

* 9 7 8 1 3 8 7 6 1 1 9 9 7 *